low

Also by Nick Flynn

low

/ poems /

nick flynn

Graywolf Press

This publication is made possible, in part, by the voters of Minnesota through a Minnesota State Arts Board Operating Support grant, thanks to a legislative appropriation from the arts and cultural heritage fund. Significant support has also been provided by the McKnight Foundation, the Amazon Literary Partnership, and other generous contributions from foundations, corporations, and individuals. To these organizations and individuals we offer our heartfelt thanks.

Published by Graywolf Press
212 Third Avenue North, Suite 485
Minneapolis, Minnesota 55401

www.graywolfpress.org

Published in the United States of America

ISBN 978-1-64445-259-2 (paperback)
ISBN 978-1-64445-260-8 (ebook)

2 4 6 8 9 7 5 3 1
First Graywolf Printing, 2023

Library of Congress Control Number: 2022952329

Cover design: Kapo Ng

Cover art: Nick Flynn

for you, at last

TRACKS

Oh, can you hear that sweet sweet sound
Yeah, I was lost but now I'm found
Sometimes there's nothing left to save
That's how you sing amazing grace

—low

side one

UNBROKEN

As if the past were riding up to meet you
as if the past could ride a horse

as if the past were a horse wandering riderless
along a dusty road

as if the horse had never been ridden

/

They say a horse is broken when the rider
can stay on

they say the past is broken when you can
let go of it

I have broken with the past, she says

I have erased it from my phone
I have blindered my eyes from her eyes

/

I didn't know the past was made of horses
I didn't even call it a horse until now

I didn't even call it strange
until I looked back on it

the past was a horse crossing a desert
a body draped over it

this is how we get the beloved home

/

Strange now to never hear a horse upon waking
or when out in the field

I didn't know the past would come for me
I didn't even call it the past until now

sometimes one gallops past
but no one else ever sees it

DUMBSTRUCK

I lit a candle last night
& sat before a photograph, my

mother as a teenager, her hair

a braided knot. Her eyes, after
a while, became wide

& doubled, as if her face were
superimposed on her other

face, the face

she'd make in the mirror
when no one else was

there. Her dress,

laced all the way up
her chest like stitches, as if

she'd been opened

& was now trapped inside
a suit of herself. Since

day one there's always been

two of me—the one
with eyes closed & the one

trying to keep the other alive. One
dumbstruck, the other

all in. The candle

burned itself down until it was just
a cup of wax. My mother

once told me about a friend

she had when she was a girl,
a girl her age, how quickly that

went away, how quickly she
became me.

DEAR MAGGOT,

First you are wing, then you are egg.
Then a thousand eggs. Then each egg
opens. Injured or poisoned, the creature
dragged its fur to the edge of the pond,
bent its snout to drink & never rose again.
By the time we smell it, you already live inside.
You ate your way in, starting with the eyes,
with the mouth, with the asshole—any hole
is a door. The belly now swells like a circus
tent. Inside, you perform your transformations—
bone to dust, muscle to dirt. In only a few hours
you will become winged again.

NOTES ON A MONUMENT TO ETHER

A man perches atop a pillared tower. He is seated & draped across his lap is another man, nearly naked, who seems to be unconscious.

The men are meant to represent the discovery that ether could be used as an anesthetic. The first successful demonstration of this was at the nearby Massachusetts General Hospital (where my brother was born), in a surgical theater that is now known as "the ether dome."

/

The origin of the word *ether* is akin to the Greek *aithein*, which means "to burn brightly," & to the Sanskrit *idhryas*, "of or like the brilliance of a clear sky."

/

Neither shall there be any more pain is etched into the side of the tower. It comes from the book of Revelation & points to the one place where (as far as we know) there truly is no pain—death. In this life, when it comes to pain, you can either feel it or you can numb it. Yet spend too long in that realm, wrestling with whatever it is you hope to numb yourself from feeling, & soon enough very little else will matter.

The word anesthesia is from the Greek *anaisthesia*, a lack of feeling.

/

Revelation is another word for apocalypse, which I always thought signaled the end of the world. But the word *apocalypse* comes from the Greek *apokalyptein*, "to take the cover off."

The word *revelation* comes directly from the Latin *revelare*, "to unveil, uncover, lay bare."

To uncover, in the sense that it is revealing some deeper truth.

/

In my twenties, when I lived in Boston, I would have passed this statue nearly every day, yet I didn't take it in—it never spoke to me. I never looked up to see the man lying in another man's arms, this pietà. This says something about the statue & something about me. Did I even have a deeper truth? My friend Richard, who lived with me in that abandoned strip joint, had just tested positive. I was working in the shelter, I knew everyone who slept outside by name. I knew my father's name, the way he used it as a blanket. If asked, I'd tell you the apocalypse had come a couple years earlier & now we were all walking through the ruins. Now we were walking in its shadows. Now we were painting curtains on plywood to make the abandoned buildings look lived in. But I was using the word wrong—I wasn't seeing what had been uncovered. I stopped to look at a box on the sidewalk & realized someone was alive inside it.

/

It was in Boston that I began to consider myself a poet, yet (or so) I anesthetized myself daily with whatever I could find, for most days it seemed I just felt too much (*neither shall there be any more pain*).

What I felt created a tension in my soul, for I could not transform it into words. Tension is essential for all art, yet for me, at this time in my life, it was not a useful tension. I didn't know how to use it.

Anaisthesia is the negation of the root *aesthete*, from the Greek *aisthetes*, "a (keen) perceiver." Though I called myself a poet, I was (clearly) not a keen perceiver.

/

Milton's *Paradise Lost* (1667) contains the first recorded use of *ether* in the poetic sense of "heavenly, celestial."

The word *ether* first appears before 1398, the year of Trevisa's translation of Bartholomew's *De Proprietatibus Rerum*. The etymological dictionary defines ether as the "upper regions of space; constituent substance of stars & planets." Ether was both the stuff the planets were floating in & the stuff the planets were made of.

What the planets were floating in is what we now call "dark matter"— we now admit that we know essentially nothing about it.

/

Essentially. That's another word like ethereal. It comes from the word *essence*, which also came into use sometime before 1398 (around the years *The Canterbury Tales* were being written).

Essence, from the Greek *ousia*—"being."

The general sense of *essence* as the most important or basic element of anything is first recorded in 1656 in Hobbes's translation of *Elements of Philosophy*.

Essence, see IS.

/

The main reason to take drugs is for the promise of the pain to go away.

Feeling no pain is what we used to answer, if asked how we were (*name your poison*) after a few beers.

It only becomes a problem when we take it to the point where (*to be or not to be*) there is no *is*.

/

Francis Bacon's triptych *In Memory of George Dyer* is a tribute to his lover, who took his life on the evening of Bacon's greatest (up to that point) success. Bacon's painting was influenced by his reading of T. S. Eliot's *The Waste Land*, especially the lines: "I have heard the key / Turn in the door," which Bacon represents in the central panel, in which a figure (Dyer) turns a key in a lock.

/

Let us go then . . .

/

Bacon's bodies are often cut open, dissected, flayed.

Michelangelo would cut up cadavers to learn human anatomy.

As it was illegal at the time to desecrate a body, he had to do this in secret, in a back room of the Basilica di Santo Spirito.

Santo Spirito. Holy Spirit.

An essence, something impossible to hold on to.

In the room the women come and go . . .

Michelangelo, searching for something inside us he could hold on to, something essential.

It is said that cutting these bodies open left him with a taste for nothing but bread & water.

This is a man / this is a tree this is bread.

Bread is essential, water is essential.

It is is the most basic, elemental sentence.

It is raining. It is broken. It is full. It is finished.

It is finished is one of the seven last phrases of Jesus.

It isn't is always just on the other side.

AZTEC

We cook

what the dead taught us
to cook—*try*

not to boil the milk, make sure
the blood is drained—we

grow flowers
to welcome them back. Some nights

we wait up, lay out bread,
salt . . . Your kiss,

I remember, tasted like geraniums—
I tend to say things I

later regret.

/

A mother

looks over the edge of her bed,
her newborn crawls across the rug

toward her—if he can only get there
in time . . . Listen,

can you hear it, in the playground,
just before the final bell—

the leaves like rattles.

/

      At the dollar store

I found a kite that didn't fly,
& eyeglasses

that made every word blur.

Did I say *word*? I meant
world.

/

      The belief

that life is a dream,
that only in death are we

truly awake, I once

felt it,
it was like pulling on a glove

that belonged to a stranger.
I found it on the sidewalk—

still warm, it was that
close.

THE UNDERNEATHEDNESS

                        Today
I misheard the word *eternity*

as *the trinity*. I was looking at

those birds falling from the sky,
thousands of them,

a photo of their corpses in
the *Times*, lined up on a white

sheet of paper, like words. *Warbler.*
Flycatcher. Swallow.

An airplane passes overhead,
then another—the cradle

is burning, creating its own
weather. *Vesper*

sparrow, violet green
swallow. Migratory—like us, they were

on their way somewhere. Maybe
it was a heat cloud, maybe

a fire tornado, maybe (like us)
they were simply starving.

From that far up
everything could fit under your

wing—when

did we become
the underneathedness to them?

side two

GOLDEN

A prayer begins & ends
each meeting, it

starts with the word *God*
& ends with the word

difference. The difference,

as far as I can tell,
between what is offered

& what is possible

is a chasm. At times it seems
we simply run out of places

to be, until we call wherever
we end up *home*,

that bright moment we
always talk about

returning to. My friend

is in the room he grew up in,
the room his grandma

died in, begging
for morphine, like all of us

will. Unlike

some of us, she begged for it
all his life. He'd find it, prepare

the needle, dim

the lights. Things got
quiet then—a bust of Jesus

on a bookshelf, translucent
yellow, like piss

or money that has been in the lake
too long. Golden,

which is how we got here
today. *God, Gold, Golem*—not

a lot of space between us.

ANEMONES

My daughter puts her face
beside a photo of her infant

self, tries to make the same
face. *All of this is a simulacrum,*

she whispers. The anemones
on the white table need

water, even though

they are, technically, dead. I
tell her the story of the guillotine, how

the head, as it rolls away,
looks back at its own body,

how the heart keeps beating
ten minutes after it is

pulled from the chest. How
if you sit before anything

long enough, it will
become something else—

that maple, say, bare
when you find it, then it brightens

to that green shimmer,
which becomes a deeper green,

& even that turns yellow, then
orange, then red.

BOYHOOD

It's like a camera—if you leave
the shutter open more

time bleeds in & with it

more light, until
their voices fill the space

you remember. If I fell—
I probably did fall, I was always

falling, into onto over
something—that enormous

rock, say, in someone's
front yard, it was the moon

& I was leaving
my footprints all over it,

it was an iceberg & I was
its doomed ship, it was

the top of a mountain, an entire
world buried below the lawn.

It was taller than a man, it had
fallen from heaven or

a spaceship, I'd climb it
when we'd visit, once a year or

so, before I ever made it inside
that house I can't remember—

I never knew who anyone was.
I was told to say *hi* so I said *hi*.

NOTES ON WANT

A car left at a stoplight in the middle of a street in a small town—the headlights still on, the driver's door open. The passenger, still in her seat, lit up by the interior light.

There is a Hindu saying: *You can get what you want, but what do you want?*

The passenger, she could lean over & pull the driver's door shut & the light would go out. She could lean over & turn the knob & the headlights would go out.

Is that what she wants, or what I want?

Where is the driver?

/

The car is oversized, American.

You had a car like that when we met, you'd bought it off your uncle, or your grandfather, you'd drive it down to the city to find me.

Everything was moving so fast then, at least that's how it seemed.

We needed to be somewhere—it might as well have been in that car.

/

As a kid, I read or dreamed or heard about astral projection. You could lay down, close your eyes, & your astral body would rise up, away from the cage of your physical body.

The astral body could travel anywhere through space & time.

It was a way out, but of what? My room? Where would I go? What did I want?

/

That woman in that car at that stoplight. Fog is coming up behind her, or maybe she is already in the middle of it—fog (like love) is something you can't see when you're in the middle of it. It creates a bubble of light around you, as everything beyond falls slowly away.

/

You lent your car to a friend & he totaled it—you let him use it & it never came back. The next time it was my turn.

The streetlight turns from yellow to red to green & back, over & over, like a song on repeat.

I borrowed a car & drove it straight to you.

/

One morning a woman—young, beautiful—approached me in the East Village. *Are you looking too?* she asked. I knew what she was saying. I could have said *yes* & we would have gone off together, in search of her want. But at that moment it wasn't my want. A couple years earlier it would have been & I would have gladly gone off with her in search of it.

/

The verb *want* came into use around 1200 (*wanten*: be lacking, be without; borrowed from Old Norse *vanta*: to want; see *wane*). The original notion of "lack" was extended to "need," & from this developed (in 1706) the sense of "desire." What happened in 1706 to transform need into desire?

/

In the movies, a woman waves out the back of the car window as it pulls away & the way she gets smaller & smaller is a slow-motion vanishing, smaller & smaller until she is gone. We know it's a trick, an illusion, we know that all along it was me who had found a way to vanish, in plain sight. To stand before you, a perfect replica, as your hands passed right through me.

/

It's dawn, no one in town is awake yet, except you. You could turn the dial on the radio until something comes back to you, a song you remember.

Am I the bad thing you were warned about?

/

Back then there was something lacking in nearly everything I touched—with you, it transformed into desire, it met yours, whenever we put ourselves in the same city. It was like the wind, how it shapes itself into whatever it encounters—just by moving toward it becomes.

/

Let's begin again—a woman waits in a car at a stoplight in the middle of a street at dawn. Maybe it's not so bad, maybe the driver will come back, bring her something sweet from the gas station—gummy worms, or vinegar & salt chips. Maybe a jug of red gasoline, if that's the problem. Maybe there is no problem—the sun just coming up, the street empty, the stores all closed.

/

The fog is coming closer now—rolling in, as they say. Maybe it's coming from a machine, maybe this is a movie set. A movie about a small town—a main street, a lunch place, a dollar store. A place you can still go to buy a padlock, a hammer. It is dawn, she is waiting. Did someone tell her to wait? Did he say he'd be right back? Did he know that she would just sit there until he came back?

Are you looking too?

/

The streetlight turns from green to red to yellow. The green is sudden, unlike the fog, which comes in slow. It makes the world outside appear as outlines, but soon even these dissolve. Is this what I want, to be inside it? To not see what blurs beyond? To smudge it with my eyes?

/

I have a daughter now, she is building a world in her computer, she leads me into it, to show me her storehouse of weapons, the garden that needs no sun, a box of chickens, a shield that can kill. Each day we get a few minutes together, mostly it's the two of us staring into the fridge, wondering if there is anything we could possibly eat. *I have a cellar full of carrots*, she tells me.

/

In an alley, a dog has found a bone, but to us it's only the sound of it, slowly wearing away beneath his teeth. The fog is seeping into everything now.

/

The car could sit here for another hour, no one will notice because no one is yet awake.

The interior light is still on, which makes a snowglobe of the car.

Your house is made of fog, your childhood is made of fog, your mother held you with hands of fog.

The town is still dark, but there you are, as the light turns from lack to need to desire, as the wind takes the shape of you.

HOTHOUSE

I whisper your name

& a garden appears, a hot-
house, all glass &

sun, the plants alone
in their pots, not part of anything

larger than themselves. Unless
you get it in the earth,

whatever is inside will die. You
carried me until I grew

too big to carry, it was
a dream & you were

the lining of that dream—
if we speak of it, it will

vanish. I

want you to carry me across
the marsh & beyond the broken

houses, but I hate that I have
to ask. It makes the grass

shimmer.

PARABLE

A great while ago the world began. People, at first, were made
of clay, like little gray dolls. The only trees were the apples we
were forbidden to eat. We would have done anything just to have
someone to talk to, but it all went away so quickly. It was carried
past us, as if the whole thing had been a play, or a traveling circus.

THE CELLARS

My brother believes he's invisible,
        but I see him everywhere. Think
of that photo: a shirtless man, bees

crawling over his chest, his neck,
his face. He wears them like jewels—
        you can't help but stare.

If he holds still nothing bad will ever
        happen. My brother, once
the world spoke to him, everything in it

was alive. Once he could spend hours
        arranging leaves on the driveway.
When the wind came it was simply

        part of what he was
building—he was the wind. Yesterday
he gave me a bill for work

        I didn't ask him to do, hours on
a piece of paper—when I ask him
to break it down, I get this:

        birds 10 hours
        trees 7 hours
        pond 12 hours

I don't know what he did with the birds or
the trees or the pond—it all looks
        the same. As kids

our house let the weather in & sometimes
        the food in the fridge went bad. In
the pantry, a silver gallon can marked

        —PEANUT BUTTER—

(a gift from the government) unopened,
        we never threw it out, just
in case. Winter, I'd be the one sent

down into the crawlspace with a torch
to thaw the pipes, setting fire to spiderwebs
        blocking my way, using my elbows

        like flippers to move me
along. Think of my family as Atlantis,
        one day here, the next day gone.

My mother, I mean. Our father, he
        lingered, I still have his ashes, I want
my brother to make a painting with them,

a book with all the pages blank. He never
        met our father—to him he was
like the sun, if he looked too long

        he'd go blind. My brother—one day
here, the next day there. He keeps
his bins in our cellar, stacked &

        numbered, he knows what's
inside each. Bin 24 holds three hundred
        disposable lighters, to be bartered

when the shit hits the fan, when it all goes
south. How, I ask, will you know it has all
　　　gone south? He just smiles. Bin 56:

hundreds of half-used tubes of toothpaste.
　　　I remind him how we used to run out &
mom would give us baking soda—

　　　sometimes she gave us salt
to sprinkle on our toothbrushes. The supply
chain is broken, he tells me—*soon*

　　　won't be any baking soda. Think
of that one silver can in the back of the pantry—
dirt wants seed, seed wants water. Take

any piece of it away & it becomes a ghost.
　　　One day (true story), I went to the bank
& the machine gave me nothing.

　　　One day, I only had half a tank
& my house was five hundred miles
　　　away. I held up my hands to the sky

& said *stop*. I put my palms together
　　　for it to go on. Everyone has a house
they are trying to keep from falling,

　　　　everyone has someone
they are trying to keep alive. Where we
are from, the bars close on Sunday

& the churches open. My people call it
a day of rest—no seed in the ground,
　　　no crops to harvest. Our cellars

let the rain seep in
but it is not water we can drink. What
will I do if my brother falls? I know

he is steady, I call him eternal—he never
        changes. He is the noise
the truck makes backing up (*beep beep,*

        beep beep, beep beep)—

        it is meant to wake us. My eternal,
his shoes made of ice, my brother,
        inside the song

only we remember. I never saw the sun
look so cold. I would offer him my jacket
        if I could reach it.

side **three**

CANARY

Your bible tells us that the Lord knows
why every bird falls. It isn't for lack of want—
their song is *seed seed seed*. A canary's
heart beats faster than light, fill a room
with them & it will glow. I once held a bird
in my hand, I once held a man in my arms.
I once let a doctor cut her way inside me
so I could live a little longer. Each was me,
circling myself, unable to land. As if I was
an astronaut & woke one morning in deep
space to nothing but silence. Here's me,
beaming frantic signals back to earth, *come*
in, Earth, come in. Each cell in our bodies
is like this astronaut, each reacts the same
way—the moment we die, the cells want to
hold on. It takes a few hours or a few days
(*our hair still grows in our coffins, fingernails*
long when they dig us up) to understand
(*heart brain blood / stopped quiet cold*).
This morning I tell my daughter we are
canaries in a coal mine, I don't know why
I tell her this—maybe the radio was playing
"Another Ice Shelf Gone." Do you know what
a coal mine is? I ask. It's a hole, she says,
where they get the coal. The miners work in
darkness, lights strapped to their foreheads,
digging into walls. A canary is a tiny light in
search of seed. Why would the miners bring
a canary down into that hole? To hear it
sing, she answers.

NOTES ON A CALENDAR FOUND IN A STRANGER'S APARTMENT

Days x'ed out in red marker.

/

The only day that isn't x'ed out is the day he died (& now, of course, all the days after).

/

Walking home, some neighbors I know are laying his books out on the stoop—*Mapplethorpe, Virginia Woolf*—to let the neighborhood absorb as much as it can. I help for a while, organizing titles by subject, then they say I should go inside, see the place.

/

Everything he owns is being carried past me & out into a pile growing beside a waiting truck. From his front door, I can almost see my front door.

His name taped to the bell.

Then I am standing in his kitchen.

/

The landlord asks if I knew him.

I say *no*.

Then he asks if I want his flatscreen.

/

Each x starts in one corner of a square of day & then fills it completely, as if to say we will never return. It is a graveyard of red crosses, a field you only visit once a year with a fistful of daisies, the ones she loved.

/

Above this graveyard of days is an image from before I was born, something you'd see tacked to the wall in the office of the guy who fixes your car—a woman in a one-piece bathing suit, leaning against a car, holding an enormous wrench.

/

Consider a spider at the center of its web, waiting. Consider the proposal to build the chimneys taller (so the ash falls elsewhere). Consider the images we see on tv—apartment buildings reduced to rubble, rooms filled with swirling scraps of paper—unpaid bills, unfinished letters—drifting through the windows like snow. All these x's.

/

It's a day where it is hard to get warm, where it is hard to know if I am sick or just sad. The past two years there have been many such days, the way it touches everything.

Car, woman, wrench.

A wrench so large it could open the universe & peel the scrim back to reveal the source of the light that shines through the holes punched into the night.

/

At some point he moved into this apartment. He went to the market when he ran out of food, he bought books at the Strand. He gathered wherever he went & brought whatever it was back here.

The neighbors told me it was a stroke, so I imagine the blood stayed inside him & was carried out with him.

Now, standing in his kitchen, I wonder how long it took to find him.

/

When the envelope that was his body was opened, the instant the thorn found that vessel in his brain, all these words drained onto the page.

/

As a kid, I was told that blood was blue inside us, that it only turns red when exposed to the air.

I still don't think this is true.

/

He was in his late sixties. His apartment rent-controlled. He lived alone.

Now I am standing in the days since, the days that followed, the days not x'ed out.

I don't want his flatscreen.

/

Under my feet, a Polaroid amidst the scattered papers—a man in a gray sweater, jeans & sneakers. He is in a chair, one leg crossed over the other knee, hands folded in his lap, a mirror of the way I sit, trying not to take up too much space.

He is looking at a woman who props her head up with her fist, the room they are in is the 1970s—a plant hangs in a window from a basket woven out of jute.

He has a mustache, she is looking at something on the floor, far away.

/

I tell myself this is my neighbor & that the woman is his sister. I tell myself the sister died a few years after this Polaroid was taken. This is why he held onto it, I tell myself, why it rose up from the debris to meet me—it was something he kept close.

/

Some postcards are stuck to his fridge with magnets—no one has disturbed the fridge, not yet. Some of the magnets are familiar works of art—"Ceci n'est pas une pipe." A can of Campbell's tomato soup. Basquiat's face. Betty Boop.

Under some of the magnets are words salvaged from fortune cookies:

> *stop searching forever, happiness is just next to you*

> *no man ever became great by imitation*

> *you will soon have the opportunity to improve your finances*

I want to open the fridge, but it feels too intimate.

/

The landlord tells me that my neighbor has a brother who lives across town—Manhattan, maybe—but this brother told the landlord to throw it all away. He didn't even come to see it first.

If you don't have the receptors, that part of the world simply doesn't exist.

/

I've had a recurring dream—a silent man sits in a chair . . . that's the whole dream.

I cannot get him to speak.

What is it you need to say? my therapist asks.

I tell him the story of how as a kid I'd find the hidden key to each summer house in my neighborhood (in a flowerpot, in the mailbox, it's never that hard). I didn't want to take anything, I'd just go inside, sit in one of their soft chairs.

I wanted to be surrounded by their things.

HIVE

Inside this there is no up,
each chamber the exact size
of a thought, big enough
to sleep in. For these few
moments, head-to-head,
we can feel our thoughts
move in & out of each other.
Here's one now: we are driving
cross-country, the country is
America, there is so much I
want to tell you, too much
about what's behind us, not
enough about what's ahead.
We cannot keep our hands
off each other, as if we could
mold each other's bodies into
the shape of this car. This car
is home, the hive is home,
the road is home, your arms
are home, the flickering bulb
in the hallway that needs
replacement, *home.*

LILITH

At first there were only two of us
—a man, a woman—we lived in
a garden, we were both made
of clay. I wandered beyond the walls
& refused to come back. Out-
side a tiger was eating a deer—
this made sense: the deer runs,
the tiger chases. Inside, when
we'd sleep, something slept on
my chest, it kept me breathing—
that's the story I chose to believe
until I didn't. Now I'm floating
on my back as if I'd fallen from
a three-story building onto the
roof of a car. My eyes have just
opened, the morning light hits
the staircase in a familiar way,
lighting the way down. I worry
the lamp is still plugged in, how
electricity in water can find you.
Let's do the math—at some point
he replaced me, they had a few
kids, one slit another's throat,
those that lived had to sleep
with their brothers, their sisters,
to make more kids, it was the
point of everything, it wasn't
ideal. I don't want to talk about
this anymore. In the river, we
lay our friends on their backs
to say goodbye as they drift
away. If they ask to be burned,

we burn them. I am asking you
to save one piece of me from
the flames. A relic. I have it here—
a tooth pulled from my head
after it split in two. A child can
carry the self forward, but so can
a tooth. Or a stonewall. Spend
some time with a stonewall—
how many hands touched it
before it found you?

PRAYER

You claim that a person who begs
is praying

& that a person who prays
begs. It's not

your fault, you never
knew me, outside so long

the hole I left behind was like
those trees at the edge

of the field, each

made of nothing
but air. I was never the type

you'd invite inside, mostly I'd just
appear at your door—

who could keep up
with that? Tonight, I'm working

the shelter, I feel loved,

I give out bed tickets
in exchange for it—*a plate of food,*

a piece of floor, a corner
away from the baseball bats.

We are all made of what
we are not.

PIETÀ

At first it was unacceptable—
strangers dressed in black,
walking away or toward a hole
in the ground, each a version
of you. Seven hundred reasons
to dig holes in the earth—some
look for water, some need a
fence. Some for this seed,
some for that body (*my god,
your body*). When you died I
didn't cry or even think of it as
change—the air didn't change.
The clocks stayed lit. Trees
had more trees hidden inside.
I'd thought of you as dead for
years, I think of everyone as
dead, moving through this ghost
world, walking a tree-lined path,
dressed in black, the memory of
a lover as strong some days as
the lover beside me. As a child,
so many went away—first the
dogs, mostly, the pets, then a
distant uncle, then a neighbor,
then it came for my friends. It was,
at first, unacceptable. I could not
keep anything alive. Yet it always
seemed you were still here, I'd pick
up the phone, I'd lay it back down,
sitting in my car at a rest stop in
the rain, the wipers intermittent—
I can't remember when it rained

this hard. We're not going any-
where, not in this. Dirt is just
the dead waiting to be reborn,
as anything—as a thought, as
a stone. As this thought. *Bring me
the powder made of emptiness*—
the Zen teacher offered this koan,
I guess he thought it would help.
Unacceptable. The earth goes on
forever, from your room you could
set out & spend your whole life
walking toward it. At some point
you will stop, catch your breath,
& this will become *home.* Inside,
a mother will hold her naked son
across her lap, nothing left to feed
him, he is just his body now, now
she does not even remember
how he came to be.

SATELLITE

We wanted to fit in, but we never
fit in, our car

gave us away, not enough
money inside

to hide. Television was
furniture, a wooden cabinet

full of tubes
& voices—it made us

laugh. Outside
the trees looked dipped in acid—

desperate gray sky, easy
to climb—

when the sun peeked out
all those branches became

migraines. The doctor up

the street, you could bring her
any wound, she'd

stand across the room
& whisper, *Can you hear me?*

Drunk, I said things
unforgivable, each word still

out there, satelliting,
beeping

like a broken star. How
strange that this

grew out of that.

CHORUS

Winter, the ground will not open,
a candle becomes her body. Ash

drifts from its wick, my coat
opens to take her inside. It's

the tail end of her last run, my mother
stands in an empty church

singing, her voice one of hundreds

of voices, a chorus of everyone
who isn't here. Hundreds

of candles, each flame a soul. Inside
this burning, darkness

holds the shape of a church
long after the church is gone.

side **four**

A WALL OF HONEY

This was the plan: we'd travel the world,
buying jars of honey wherever we went—
this one from Vietnam (*nearly black*),
this one from Egypt (*golden, milky*). It
all depends, of course, on the flowers.
Back home, I'd build a wall of these jars,
sit at a wooden table, watch as the sun
poured through. *Home* . . . I was always
walking toward it, with what they call
the "key" in my hand. I thought home
was where the dead gather, like amber,
a bug you can buy to hang from your
neck. This is what I learned: to make it
home, you must carve a door for the dead,
paint a number on it, so she'll know
where to find you.

CATACOMB

My name comes from a man I
never knew, his name comes
from a man he never knew, it
goes like that all the way down
until the thread is lost. It
comes from the Irish word *flan*—
meaning ruddy, or red-faced.
The landlord stands in his manor,
looks out over his fields, no,
Little Lord Go Fuck Yourself
never saw his fields, his middle-
man collected the rent, from
the peasants, the red-faced,
the *flan*. Now I spend hours
at the sink, water running over
my hands. How long will it last?
The window looks out at a brick
wall, the sun moves tiny shadows
across the grout, I can almost reach out
& hold it. My daughter carries this
same name, peasant child, I didn't
know what else to do with it. That
name, like a ghost, calling out from
all that light. This window once
looked out over a meadow, all those
people we had to kill to make room
(*multiply that by a city, divide that by
the amount of gold in Hispaniola*).
We came here to get away, we
were hungry, we had to prove our-
selves, the new landlord nodded in
their direction, we knew what we had

to do. It's hard to think how to set this right. We could move all the bones into the spare room (if we had a spare room), arrange them in a way that showed respect. What I need to do now is help my daughter with her algebra. *Peggy rode her bike to the farm. Mike decided to go by car. It took Mike half an hour to get there. Peggy made the trip in two hours. If Mike was traveling thirty-six miles per hour faster than Peggy, how far is the farm?* The idea is to find out what you don't know by looking at what you know. Let's start by naming what we know—*everyone is trying to get back to that farm.*

THE DAY THE EARTH STOOD STILL

Field, rust, stone. Each night you
return to the same place—a woman

lies naked in a field, the way her
body holds itself tells you the way

she would hold you. She floats on
the grass, each blade has roots

reaching to the rivers below. *Hidden,*
that might be the word, she might be

your mother, or the lover you will meet
in twenty years. Or is it just her body,

laid out in that field, has she already
gone? The universe grows smaller

every day, now she's a stone you visit
once a year or so, knowing that beneath

your knees the skeleton of her whitens
in a box. Why do bones last forever

when this thought vanishes so
quickly? Look

into the night, there must be
millions like you, each looking back

at us. Maybe we are all speaking to each
other, maybe we are showing you how

we want to be held.

WATER CYCLE

All the rain in the world

is falling, making
a door you can't open. On

one side of this door, your
body—you are inside it

now. On

the other side, your other
body, the one

you've been trying to enter
since you were born. To find

yourself, you must cross
this threshold of rain. Each

drop whispers, *You*

will not be this beautiful
forever—one day

you will grow so luminous
this world will not be able to

contain it. As a newborn
you were held close

to your father's chest, to imprint
his smell upon you. Where did he

go? From here,

you can almost make him out,
the *you* you wanted to be,

though he's more a silhouette
than a hand you could

hold. Careful

now, a hole has opened at
your feet, all the rain spiraling

down it, nowhere else

to go, like that chart
on the wall in elementary school

—THE WATER CYCLE—

how it leaps from liquid to gas
to solid to teardrop to

icicle to steam to waterfall to
piss, an arrow

connecting each. Nothing

is ever lost, no one is ever
unlost. Besides, it hurts to have

skin to pour a soul into.

SACRED TRASH

My daughter scribbles out
a stranger's face in the news-

paper—maybe

she saw something in his eyes,
something she didn't want

to see. It's

a black cloud now, I saved it,
I cannot seem to throw it

away—whatever
a hand touched could be

the word of God. Go in-

to the desert with your shovel,
dig anywhere & you will find

a crypt. Inside, all the scraps
of paper the people could

gather—*grocery list,
brick invoice, workers'*

*names . . . the torn beginnings of what
we now call "gospel"*—

all of it, like time, flattened. It was
the beginning, no one knew what

was worth saving, or whose hand
made anything

sacred. Nothing

has changed. My daughter
draws a picture of the two of us,

side-by-side, our arms wide—
this is what I'll remember,

I tell myself.

MARRIAGE

I was married once, at least
we thought about it, it was in
b&w, we were tiny, walking
in a forest, the trees dwarfed
us—the trees had been married
forever, moss hung from their
fallen branches, we had to
step over them. We put on
the costumes—*groom, bride*—
these are jobs, I realized, that
only last a couple hours. Why
not try it, what could we lose,
we were already deep inside
the forest, we were already lost,
marriage was just where the path
was headed—I thought it would
make us more like the trees,
growing closer every year. I
wanted you to put your hand
out, to pull me closer, I wanted
all the way in. A child would be
the glue. Was it wrong to think of
a child as glue? Too late, we were
already in our costumes, we'd already
had a shower, maybe someone
would give us a red toaster. It was
just another day to get through,
even if it felt like everyone was
talking through long cardboard
tubes. In the distance, the Empire
State Building, no matter where
we were we could find a window

or a roof & it would be lit up red
or blue or green & that would
tell us what month we were in.
We could even climb it (it's not
impossible) & then look back
at all the windows we had looked
at it through, all over the city,
waking up in strange rooms,
& there it was, waiting. It was
the tallest for a while & then
it wasn't & then it was again.

NOTES ON CORONA (YEAR ONE)

(february)

Snow woke me, flakes so
white I felt

blind. *Sometimes*

*we don't like the angels God
sends,* the preacher

preached (*this one
wears a crown, this one is*

a thorn). My daughter
wanted to go, so I typed

"church" into Yelp
& took her. The choir

was small, but enough
to fill us. *You have heard,*

no doubt, of my earlier life.

(march)

My earlier life was something
I held inside &

tried to destroy

before it could destroy
me. A lot (*yes*) was taken for

granted, often it was (*yes yes*) me
who took it. In every

field now we are building
rooms made of air—we call them

thresholds. *Where is*
everyone? you ask, as your voice

echoes across the emptiness,
as everything slowly

unplugs.

(march)

I had to unplug my life. At each leg

the terminal was empty. I ate
a sandwich from a machine, in

long-term parking a yellow film
dusted my car. Downtown,

a man rode a shopping cart in
the middle of the street. Another

rode past on a child's bike, baring
his teeth. Is this

the way it ends—maps on tv, red
splotches blotting out

towns, home sudden
& far away? I kept a list of things to do

folded in my pocket.

(march)

This list is one you don't want
to be on. Today

the air is silent, but soon will be
loud. Today it is birds,

but soon will be sirens. *What was
here?* we ask, passing an empty

storefront. We ask, *Is* _____

still alive? but instantly
regret it. The low

flowers of spring have just
appeared, a chain of purple

pushing up from the dark (*anemone,
gentian, creeping charlie*). *See*

you on the other side (regret).

(april)

On the other side, on the tiny
screen in my palm, I see

Rome. I see the bridge I'd cross

on my Vespa, empty
now, yet overflowing, the Tevere

overflowing, a word we hear
more & more, our borders, our

streets, our hearts *overflowing*
overflowing overflowing. Once

we came this close to losing each
other. Once you

get on the machine it is un-
likely you will ever

get off.

(may)

Get off, we whisper, to the cop
kneeling on your neck,

his hand in his pocket,
his partner's knee

on your lungs, the whole
force lined up, all of us, all

the way down your spine.
O mama, you gasp, until

each molecule of your name
becomes you, until thousands of you

stand outside his door, offering
to help his wife pack, offering him

another beer,
before we burn his house down.

(june)

After the house across from him
burned, my friend

stood at the window behind his
daughter, looking out at

the emptiness. Trucks

outside hospitals, blocks
of ice, tents

set up in parks, as if they'd
been there since the Civil War.

Where did everyone go?

my daughter asks. This
is the world without us, comes

the answer, this is what inside
looks like.

(august)

Inside looks like nine minutes
& twenty-nine seconds. Inside

looks like the word *overflowing*
& a chain of purple pushing up

from the dark. It was Paul in
Galatians who said, *You*

have heard, no doubt, of my earlier
life. Offering

atonement, seeking
forgiveness. Now we've forgotten

what it was we were going to do

with this day. Snow
woke us, the flakes so white

they nearly blinded us.

side five

I AM A TOWN

I am a town held together by paint
one day you'll forget I exist

I am the book that no one has read
silverfish made me their home

open me up half my words gone
if you hold me I might feel intact

I am the man no one else sees
ten thousand years I've been dirt

skateboarder kids live on the beach
their piano lives under a tarp

everyone struggles just out of sight
we leave & come back like the tide

is there a song that can keep us intact
by august the streets smell like piss

this is the year that no one was born
this is the year no one died

I am a house no one else wants
I'm the man asking for smoke

the rains will come & the water will rise
the sun gets closer each day

I'm the parade & I'm the tattoo
put everything lost inside me

NOTES ON A PHOTOGRAPH FROM 1884

So much has been forgotten—entire libraries burned, a graveyard of statues on the edge of every city.

Muddy fields, dirt roads, torn boots.

A man walks into the woods & three months later he walks out, leading two bears on leashes, their snouts muzzled. Up on their hind legs they are taller than the man, yet (seemingly) all he has to control them is a stick.

How he got the muzzles on them he does not say.

/

Children line the boardwalk to watch them dance—that's what he calls it, though they are not dancing.

One child says:
>   That one looks like it's wearing a bear suit, the way its fur hangs off it—it's as if someone wrapped a bear coat around a little bear, to keep it warm.

/

The street is made of dirt, it sometimes seems everything is made of dirt. Place your hand on the earth & feel its pulse. If you are tired there are fields.

/

Somedays it's as if I took everything that hides inside me & put it on the outside & now it walks beside me on a leash, broken somehow. You stop to say hi, you pretend not to notice—I'm trying to warn you.

/

I once saw a woman crossing a field, carrying a loaf of bread in the basket of her bicycle. The air was soft, the sun was low. It was France, there were no animals to disturb her because all the animals had been eaten a hundred years ago. You could plant a garden & nothing would come in the night to devour it.

Here, it's not like that, not yet. Here, the eyes of everything we haven't eaten line the edges of every field. Even this road, it was made by night animals, who found their way from the river. It was made by the feet of all those who came before & stayed, hidden.

/

I don't know what the truth was before this. I know when those libraries burned we forgot how to build domes made of stone. We forgot how to coax bees into our hives. We forgot how to capture a bear & then let it walk beside us.

Yet someone knew to carve footpaths into roads. Someone built a building out of wood, then someone built another one next to it, &

on & on. Someone made shoes, someone sold flour, until we'd emp-
tied the land of all danger.

Then came the man leading two bears on leashes.

/

This is how he might have done it: In the middle of the woods is a
clearing, & in this clearing stands an oak. Honeybees made a hive
in a hollow of this tree & this hive is now heavy with honey. The
man can see claw marks in the dense bark, he can imagine the bear
reaching up. This is where he will hang a heavy cage from a branch,
set it to fall when the bear steps beneath it. It will take a month to
lure the bear under, for the trap to fall. Inside, the bear will search
for a way out, raise his paws, shake the bars, roar. For a month, the
man will have to push food toward it with a stick—at first even this
stick will be eaten. After a month the bear will allow the man to
lay a hand on his head as he eats—cage anything long enough & it
will give up. Another month & the man is able to reach in & slip the
muzzles on & open the cage.

/

A child thinks:
> Who wouldn't want to keep a bear on a leash? You could walk into
> any town a stranger & no one would try to stop you.

What do we have that even comes close to that wildness?

/

Some throw coins, some just listen. A woman laughs from an open window. A door slams. Then another. Then silence, as if everyone were holding their breath, as if everyone were dead, but only for a few long minutes. Painful, this silence, because it isn't really there. That's when you hear what lives beneath silence, the sound that's always there. Is it the earth coming apart? Is it the blood in your ears, pressing against the dark?

/

We all have an animal that's trying to get out from inside us, we're all bears wearing the skins of humans, we're all animals who have simply forgotten our claws.

Everything hides inside us—once it would only come out at night, but lately it has been appearing in daylight.

Listen, it is breathing for me now.

It swallows every sound I make.

NINETEEN EIGHTY-FOUR

You crawled last night in
through my window,

don't you want this?

you whispered. Your robe
hung on a nail, your name on

a piece of cardboard
tacked to the wall. What lives

inside us

is monstrous, it comes out
of our mouths at

night, sometimes

as a song, sometimes as
a word, the word used to pry

the jar open, the word bees
sing in the hive. I told you

how I'd climb to the roof
& toss appliances into the burned-

out shell next door—*dead
refrigerator, dead stove, dead*

washing machine—silent

as they fell. I woke up one day
with nowhere to be, cold

pizza in the backseat, my pickup
sideways in the driveway. I built

that truck around me, I tried to
warn you, I tried to warn

everyone.

FORGETFULNESS

The camera that photographed the sun
melted, its last picture is shadowless,
a wisp of yellow rising from the brighter
yellow. Everything on earth grows from
this yellow—like God, look at it & you will
go blind. Maybe the sun is God, if God
is where everything comes from. Some
mornings still I wake up before dawn
& just wait for it. I used to wake up with one
word coming out of me (the word was *fuck*),
my eyes not yet open. I had a joke about
shaking my tiny fist at the sky, yet some
days still I shook it—*happily ever after*
didn't mean forever. Before the latest surgery
I asked, What will you give me? *Propofol*,
the nurse smiled—*the same thing that killed
Michael Jackson*. We both laughed—*Nothing
but the best*. The needle inside, three
lightbulbs over my head, how long before
I'm gone? Roll onto your side, she mur-
mured, then there I was, a black crystal
spiderweb draping each word. All this
light I tried to tell her, comes from the sun.
Did you see the photographs—the camera
melted, yellow, like the skin of a tropical
fruit. The entire plane applauded when
the pilot found the earth again.

0000

Euclid had what we now call *horror of the infinite*, that
something—anything—could simply go on & on. Those
years I lived in bars were like that (*unbounded, indefinite*)
but I feared more the me outside those walls. Now I'm
back—a woman on the stool beside me smiles. I'm not
drinking, just waiting for some takeout, wearing a shirt
with infinity (*an 8 asleep on its side*) stitched onto the back.
As the woman returns from the john, she runs a finger
along my shoulder & says, *I like your infinity shirt*. She
then shows me her inner forearm, a tattoo that looks
like four Os laid beside each other—*OOOO*—the middle
two overlapping. *A double infinity*, she whispers, as if
it were a car waiting outside. What does it mean
to have twice as much of what is already terrifying?

VOLUNTEERS

From a distance the city
looks blanketed in

smoke—inside,

it's hard to breathe. A song
is playing, the walls

are spattered with, *what
is that, oil?* That

soldier, this isn't

his house, it wasn't his sister.
The explosion, it

came from somewhere
outside of him, it was

called in. This house,

if we can empty it of all
meaning,

we will be safe. What about
the house next to it

& the house next to that? That
song has been playing this whole

time, an almost

imperceptible drone. *The family?*
They live in a camp now.

The student? She
didn't finish her assignment.

The patient? He's on life-
support. *The garden?* Seed

blew in from fields
a hundred miles away.

OUR FRIENDS BECOME FLOWERS

alone in a field / we open our knives
the names of our friends are fading

allium frog's foot / gold cup jewelweed
lowlands don't always heal

/

sun pours into flesh / flesh pours into dirt
the dirt worms work into air

an army of flowers / girls use them for swords
to leave the fields so broken

/

believe in the sun / it will never die
believe that the rain will keep falling

this spaceship this seed / it moves us through time
the cure all along grows beside us

BIRDLAND

Life, child, does a number on us,
& this number opens a door. Birds
find their way in—*birdhouse, doll-
house, dreamhouse*—we make
ourselves small so we can fit in-
side. From the sink I can see that
spot beyond the tree line where we
bring the bones, far enough from
the house so the rats, always looking,
won't come close. By morning they
are gone. Look up, thousands of hungry
shadows, a migration, each having
come a distance we call *impossible*,
following a river in the sky we call
invisible. They can't mourn us
the way we mourn them, our palms
pressed together, made of light. Do
they know that everyone they love
will also die, or do they forget.
The dead, I mean, not the birds.

side **six**

KRAKOW

I thought I'd come to the end
of something, but the end is not

a place you visit, not

a train you either get off
or stay on—it spreads outward

from wherever you find your-
self. The summer

Blade Runner was rereleased, I

watched it on an enormous
screen, leftover from the communist

era (*I've seen things*

you people wouldn't believe). I
wasn't eating meat, but I'd lost

the words for vegetables. I'd go
to milk bars & just point—*Szpinak.*

Ziemniak. Kawa. I

waited in line to buy a can of
something from a grocery store—

a smiling girl on the label,

some words I could not read.
I placed it in the center of

my empty room &
imagined what was inside. If

I never opened it

it could be anything. The girl
on the label could be inside, or

a key to another room, or
a series of smaller cans, each

with its own mystery

on the label. It might never
end. Sometimes

you go to the well & the well

is empty, sometimes
you turn on the faucet

& nothing comes. You have
a choice—drink the nothing

or wait a little longer.

I missed my train to Oświęcim,
but caught the next one. At

sundown I wandered the ruins
& found a blackberry growing

from a pile of ash. *Holy*, I thought,
but could never find a way

to get inside it.

BIKINI

We grew up inside a bomb,

we tested it on an island
we'd emptied of people. In

the photograph, dwarf

warships circle a crown
rising up from the waves—we knew

what happened

to the other creatures who
lived on that island,

all of us knew. Some of us
just fit into darkness,

make it whole. Since

that day, a small red dot
hangs in the air, whenever

we close our eyes, wherever
we turn our heads, it's

always there, small & red.

FILM

It's the scene where the young single mother goes
into a food pantry & is walked through the aisles
& given a couple bags of whatever she wants
but at some point she is alone & she turns her body
into a corner & pulls the lid off a can of what looks
like baked beans & pours them into her hand &
starts to shovel them into her mouth until
the woman who had shown her such terrible
kindness comes back & touches her arm softly
& asks if she's okay, but the mother, dazed, says
only *I'm sorry I'm sorry I'm sorry*. I'm on the couch
beside my daughter, *What's happening?* she asks
& I start to cry but not so much that she can hear.
She's hungry, I say, *she's hungry*.

ANCHOR

If you fill your house with water,
it will, at some point, push all the
windows out. It will seep through
the seams, where the door meets
the frame, then it will open the door.
From the sidewalk it will look like
a fountain, the lawn now thick with it,
the membrane between air & water
dissolved. Can you imagine what it's like
to become all of one thing? That
tunnel they all talk about, the one
you enter on your way out, it is
carved through stone, surrounded
by water, & the water is leaking in.
Stretch out your hands—it is rushing
past you, up to your ankles now, it pulls
you along, it's going where you are going.
How long can you hold your breath?

NOTES ON THORNS & BLOOD

It's mostly our hands, when we take off our gloves.

It's mostly our legs, when we come in from the fields—red lines tattooed across blue veins.

We try to keep it inside but it comes out—the knife slips, the bruise rises. Thorns, mostly, they catch on our skin as we pass. Our hands press down, in case it's more, in case it's deeper, our fingers to our mouths, we try to keep it inside by swallowing.

/

These short days of December erase everything, the carols in the drugstore remind us—we can't escape it. What did we come in for? *Band-Aids? Aspirin? A test to show us how sick we are?* I don't want to be the reason someone else dies—that's why I'm in the fields again, alone, hacking away at the buckthorn, the Japanese honeysuckle, the multiflora rose.

/

The rose is thick with thorns, their tendrils reach out eight, ten feet, wrapping around themselves, making it hard to get at the root ball.

The sky is a gray stone dangling over my head.

The fields have been plowed, rainwater caught in each trough, reflecting the sky. The farmer complains about the stones, how they rise up no matter how often he plows.

He walks before the tractor, tossing them into the bucket.

A thorn finds my thumb, I take off my glove—blood comes out of its little hole.

/

In his painting *The Beheading of Saint John the Baptist*, Caravaggio places himself in a cell, his face pressed against the bars, watching. John's eyes are closed; neither he nor his executioner are wearing shirts, or much of anything. A woman holds a platter, another woman holds her hands to her face. A red cloth is draped over John's waist, a mirror of the blood flowing from the wound in his neck. Caravaggio signed his name to the painting (the only time he will ever sign his name to a painting) using the blood flowing from the wound. As if he'd escaped his prison for a moment to say, *I was here.* The executioner presses John's head to the ground with one hand; he hides the knife behind his back in the other. John the Baptist is about to become pure energy—this is what is meant by *resurrection.* No one comes back, not as they were. In this instant the body will transform into what it once was & what it could be—an empty chair, a snake with its mouth stuck open, a blue marble pressed inside it.

/

Lili calls out from the kitchen door, *You ready?*

Ready for what, I wonder.

/

I look at the sky—it will be cold now until May, no end to the cold, each day colder. The map on my phone shows it coming, a blue mass of cold.

/

I cut another tendril. Jung observed how sap, imitating blood, *cycled through the seasons, flowing down to its earthbound roots in winter & returning as fruit in summer.* Like us, the plants try to keep it inside, but it keeps coming out. The knife slips. If I could, I'd let it flow into the dirt & ask it to stay.

/

In Old English, the word for blood (*blod*) would normally have been expected to change in Middle English to a pronunciation that rhymes with *food*, but in the early 1500s, the vowel was shortened to rhyme with *good*, & later with *flood*.

Food, good, flood, blood. (It is perhaps related to the root of the Old English *blowen*: to flower; see *bloom*).

Buckthorn, honeysuckle, rose.

A thorn to your wrist, a line of red blooms. In the shower you will wash it off as if it never was.

By bedtime, you won't even be able to find the holes.

THEY ARE FALLING ALL AROUND ME

We made a dance of all the ways
we'd hurt our bodies. I made a list
to read from the stage—*broken nose,*
broken ribs, broken arm, broken
cheekbone. Dance, I was told, is simply
the way a body crosses space, each
step a story of being held & falling,
held & falling. A question was asked,
How would you enter a body of water?
I closed my eyes & took a step backward.
When death entered, it became silent, we
moved into shadows—some of us refused
to touch the body. To prepare I'd been
watching some kids in an abandoned lot—
their dirtbomb war, their sticks for guns. One
lifted a branch twice his size over his head
& with it he made the other boys dance.

THE ABOUTNESS

Why
in my contacts is there a folder marked
dead people & why in the newspaper
is every car on fire? Why is everyone
just standing around as it burns? It
just happened, the caption tells us, but
doesn't everything *just happen?* Why
isn't there a newspaper that lists all of
you who have died alongside all of us
still alive? One day, the number of us
will surpass the number of you (or is it
too late for that?). We close our eyes
when the needle drops, a hard black
disc, a crackling sound—then songbirds
emerge from the cone of the Victrola,
the one the dog sat before, listening.
No one saw them coming. Lift the needle
& they all pour back into the funnel.
That's the whole trick—it's happening
in your head, it was always about listening.
Now everyone is talking about UFOs, how
real they are—declassified videos of lights
dancing in the sky, what else could they be?
We're in an airplane now over the sea,
something hovering beneath us, mirroring
us—when we dive, the mystery rises up,
when it meets us, it disappears.

BAPTISMAL

A spiderweb is not
a tool

the spider uses to catch
its prey—it *is*

the spider, stretched
outside itself. How far

beyond our fingertips
do our bodies

extend? What

is it we are suspended
over, what

holds us? Maybe
we are the reason

God made other people,
so we could wait

together, held.

BIRTHDAY

At some point the lights will go out
& a cake will appear to be floating in
the doorway & we will begin the song.
The cake will be your favorite, held aloft
by the ones who love you & it will be
on fire, an offering, one flame for each
year you've been with us. Inside each
flame, millions of smaller flames, one
for each hour & before you make your
wish you will wonder if these aren't
the candles that never go out, that
jump back to life after each breath—
some call them *tricks*, but think what
it means for the wish, that your breath,
instead of ending it, makes the flame
want to stay.

STORM

An umbrella opening like a rose,
a tree blooming like an umbrella,
this is the first night we can sleep
with the window open, this is where
we can pour ourselves—not to quiet
the silence, but to hold what we can see
a little closer. What do I see? A heat
pipe, peeling; a window, cloudy—it
has to go somewhere, this feeling.
It came before anything coalesced,
before we became this. *Family* is
a word, *home* is a word, it could have
gone either way, it could have kept
moving from the center, we would
have become something else. That
girl with the umbrella, she is my daughter,
entering into a storm. That man in
a room surrounded by his own thoughts,
that was me, but now it's you.

LINER NOTES

Epigraph (*Can you hear that sweet sweet sound . . .*) / from the song
"(That's How You Sing) Amazing Grace," by the band Low, written
by Alan Sparhawk & Mimi Parker.

"Notes on a Monument to Ether" / the lines *this is a man / this is a tree
this is bread* is from the poem "In the Middle of Life" by Tadeusz
Różewicz (translated by Czesław Miłosz); the phrase *It is finished*
came to me thanks to Pádraig Ó Tuama, who also pointed out that
it is one of the last seven words (phrases) of Jesus.

"The Underneathedness" / the title is a word encountered in the poem
"Characteristics of Life" by Camille T. Dungy.

"Golden" is for Guy Barash.

"Notes on Want" is based on a photograph by Gregory Crewdson
(*Untitled*, 2004).

"The Cellars" / the photograph mentioned is by Richard Avedon
(*Beekeeper, Davis, California, May 9, 1981*).

"Pietà" is for Richard McCann.

"Sacred Trash" / is the title of a book by Adina Hoffman & Peter Cole.

"I Am a Town" / written for, included in & providing the title for the
eponymous film, a documentary about Provincetown, directed by
Mischa Richter.

"Notes on a Photograph from 1884" / the photograph is without
attribution.

"Our Friends Become Flowers" is a collaboration with eteam (Flowers,
part 5) / Nick Flynn (poem), Guy Barash (electronics), Kathleen
Sepové (piano).

"Film" / the film is *I, Daniel Blake*, directed by Ken Loach.

"Notes on Thorns & Blood" is a collaboration with the images of
Pietro Costa, who uses the blood of his subjects to create his por-
traits. The Jung quote on sap (*cycled through the seasons . . .*) is from
an essay by Matthew Bevis, "Unknowing Lyric," in *Poetry*, 2017.

"They Are Falling All Around Me" / the title is a song by Bernice
Johnson Reagon; the poem is for Stephen Yoshen & Jeff Bliss.

"Birthday" was written for Marie Howe, on her birthday.

TAKEN

AGNI / Notes on Thorns & Blood

The American Poetry Review / Golden; Prayer; Lilith; Storm

Bennington Review / Aztec

BOMB / Notes on a Monument to Ether

The Commuter (Electric Literature) / Anemones; Marriage

descant / Hothouse; *The Day the Earth Stood Still*; Chorus

Divigations / Notes on Want

FENCE / Sacred Trash; The Aboutness

Harvard Review / OOOO

Midst / Notes on Corona (Year One)

New Ohio Review / Canary

The New Yorker / Unbroken

Oxford American / Forgetfulness; Birdland; Baptismal; Anchor

Peripheries / Krakow

Ploughshares / The Underneathedness; Pietà

Provincetown Arts / Notes on a Calendar Found in a Stranger's
    Apartment; I Am a Town; The Cellars

A Public Space / Boyhood

Revista de la Universidad (Mexico DF) / Notes on Corona (Year One)
    (Spanish translation)

Salmagundi / Notes on a Photograph from 1884

The Southampton Review / Satellite; Dumbstruck

Tupelo Quarterly / Hive

The Virginia Quarterly Review / Water Cycle; Catacomb; They Are
    Falling All Around Me

DEBTS

GRATITUDE *note*: these poems emerged from the depths of a global pandemic with a lot of help . . . that help includes WRITERS (aka students) I've been fortunate enough to work alongside, as well as: GRAYWOLF Fiona McCrae, Carmen Giménez, Katie Dublinski, Chantz Erolin, Marisa Atkinson COVER GENIUS Kapo Ng GOD'S HAND Jeff Shotts GOOD EYES Rebecca Wolff, Elizabeth Winston, Ben Terrall, Major Jackson, Elizabeth Scanlon, Michael Dumanis, Brigid Hughes, Lou Ann Walker, Bianca Stone, Kristina Marie Darling, Guadalupe Nettel, Annelyse Gelman, Brett Fletcher Lauer, John Skoyles, Rogan Kelly, Kelle Groom, Eden Werring, Sherah Bloor, Greg Pardlo, Robert Boyers, Peg Boyers, Kevin Young, Dave Wanczyk, Rebecca Gayle Howell INSPIRATION Alan Sparhawk, Mimi Parker (r.i.p.), Ryan McGinley, Laurie Anderson, Ada Limón, Nan Goldin, Sharon Olds, Haleh Liza Gafori WAGON CIRCLE Marie Howe, Donna Masini, Victoria Redel, Martin Moran, Mark Conway, Ricky Ian Gordon, Padraig Ó Tuama, Vievee Francis, Michael Klein, Rachel Eliza Griffiths, Sophie Cabot Black, Richard McCann (r.i.p.), Lili Glauber, Debra Gitterman, Mark Adams, Jacques Servin, Kate Hill STAY CLOSE Puy Navarro, Carolyn Forché, Jojo Keane, Susan Jennings, Jennifer Franklin, Hala Alyan, Natalie Klym, Simi Stone, Philip Marshall, Mischa Richter, Roberto Tejada, Caroline Crumpacker GROUND CONTROL Olena Kalytiak Davis, Pat Oleszko, Clarisse Gorokhoff, Susan Minot, Amity Stoddard, Wayne Gilbert, Lindsay Comstock, Michael Zilkha, Roger Rosenblatt, Erin Belieu, Kevin Prufer, Ann Hood, André Dubus III, Meghan Finn, Mark Wunderlich, LIFE SUPPORT Jericho Brown, Ann Christensen, Stephen Elliott, Jill Bialosky, Nancy Rommelmann, Terrance Hayes, Alison Granucci, Rebecca Makkai, Tupelo Hassman, Adam McLaughlin, Patrick McElroy, John Bowe, Jack Ortiz, Bill Arning FAMILY AFFAIR Jacqueline Woodson, Tom Johnston, Nuar Alsadir, Franc Graham, Guy Barash, Heidi Marben, Mike Quinn, Tate Sherman, Doug Montgomery, Jessica Lamontagne, Chodo Campbell, Bill Clegg, Lisa Swee, Andrew Swee, Stacey Gerrish, Tad Flynn, Lili Taylor, Maeve Lulu Taylor Flynn EMPTY WITHOUT

Nick Flynn's books include *This Is the Night Our House Will Catch Fire* (Norton, 2020); and *Stay: Threads, Collaborations, Conversations* (Ze Books, 2020), which documents twenty-five years of his collaborations with artists, filmmakers, and composers. He is also the author of six collections of poetry (all published by Graywolf), including *Some Ether* (2000) and *I Will Destroy You* (2019). His best-selling memoir *Another Bullshit Night in Suck City* (Norton, 2004) was made into a film starring Robert DeNiro (Focus Features, 2012), and has been translated into fifteen languages. He is a professor in the creative writing program at the University of Houston, where he is in residence each spring. www.nickflynn.org

The text of *Low* is set in ITC Giovanni Std.
Book design by Rachel Holscher.
Composition by Bookmobile Design & Digital
Publisher Services, Minneapolis, Minnesota.
Manufactured by Versa Press on acid-free,
30 percent postconsumer wastepaper.